*IMPORTANT
(Please Read)

This book contains six different types of blank grid sheets that should be use
find them toward the back of the book. They will be either in "portrait" or "landscape" mode and are labeled as:

Blank grid sheet #1,
Blank grid sheet #2,
Blank grid sheet #3,
Blank grid sheet #4,
Blank grid sheet #5 and
Blank grid sheet #6

There is one copy of the required blank grid sheet for each drawing included in this book that you can use directly, or you can tear it out and use it to make your own extra copies if you like.

You can also find all the blank grid sheet templates to download and print out as often as you like online for free on our website at: Magniscape.com/grids

---

*Please use the correct blank grid sheet for each drawing
according to the instructions shown at the top of each page.

At the end of the advanced images section you will find three (finished images) pages. These pages will show you what all the drawings should look like when they are completed.

Have Fun!

THIS BOOK'S CONTENTS:

- **IMPORTANT** Instructions
- Drawings #1 - #10 **(SIMPLE)**
- Drawings #11 - #20 **(INTERMEDIATE)**
- Drawings #21 - #30 **(ADVANCED)**
- **Finished Images Pages**

    Finished (Simple) Images
    Finished (Intermediate) Images
    Finished (Advanced) Images

- **Blank Grid Sheets**

    Blank grid sheet #1
    Blank grid sheet #2
    Blank grid sheet #3
    Blank grid sheet #4
    Blank grid sheet #5
    Blank grid sheet #6

Find more at: → Magniscape.com

Drawing #1 - What is it?

Instructions: Recreate the picture by copying the components below into the appropriate squares on blank grid sheet #5.

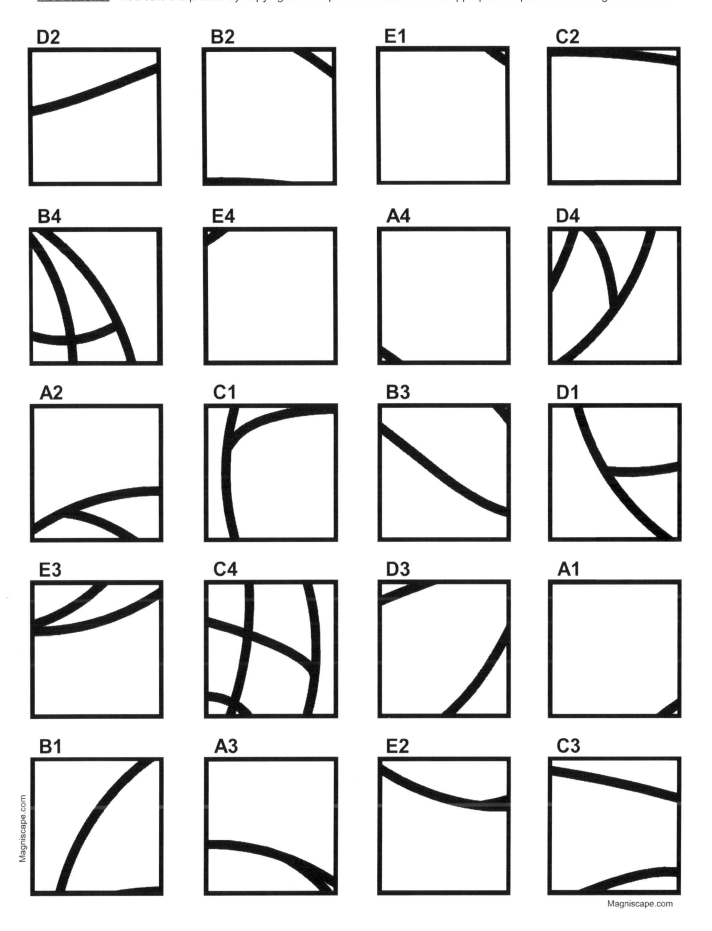

D2 B2 E1 C2

B4 E4 A4 D4

A2 C1 B3 D1

E3 C4 D3 A1

B1 A3 E2 C3

Drawing #2 - What is it?

Instructions: Recreate the picture by copying the components below into the appropriate squares on blank grid sheet #5.

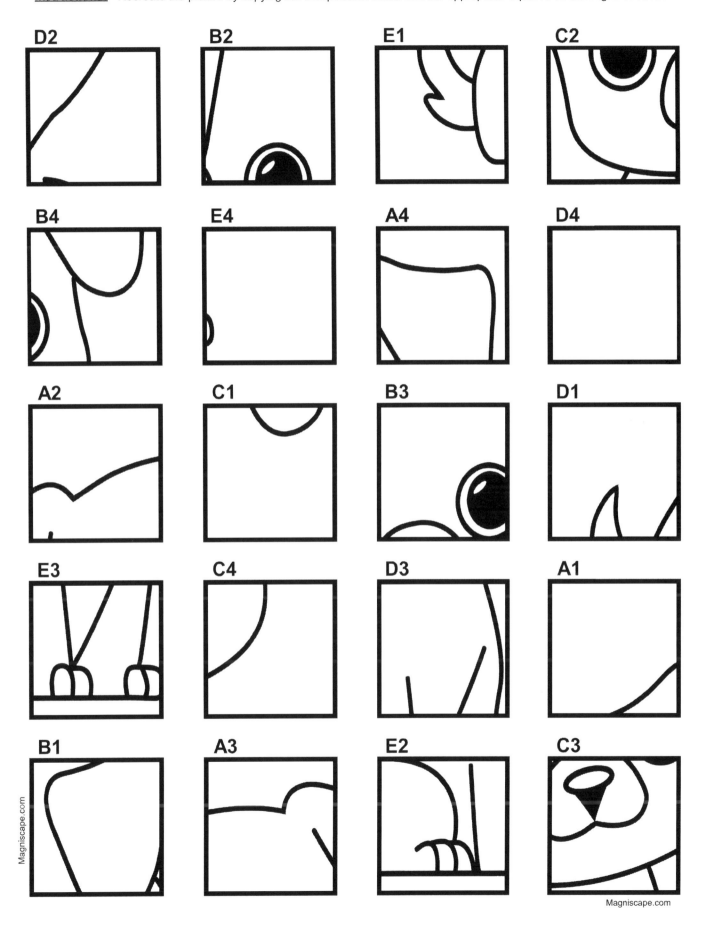

D2 B2 E1 C2
B4 E4 A4 D4
A2 C1 B3 D1
E3 C4 D3 A1
B1 A3 E2 C3

Magniscape.com

Drawing #3 - What is it?

Instructions: Recreate the picture by copying the components below into the appropriate squares on blank grid sheet #5.

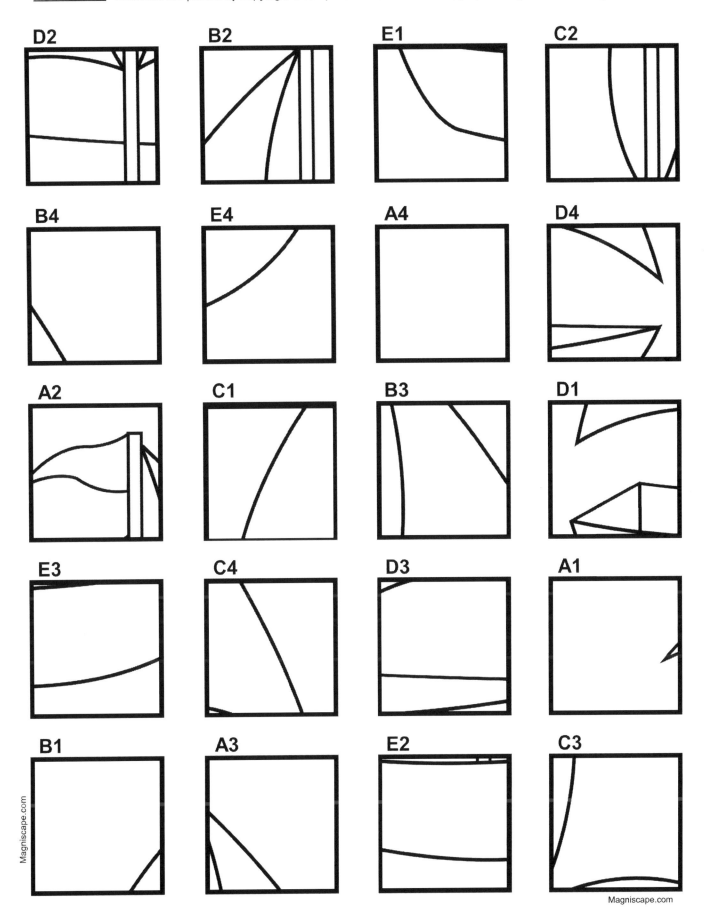

Drawing #4 - What is it?

Instructions: Recreate the picture by copying the components below into the appropriate squares on blank grid sheet #5.

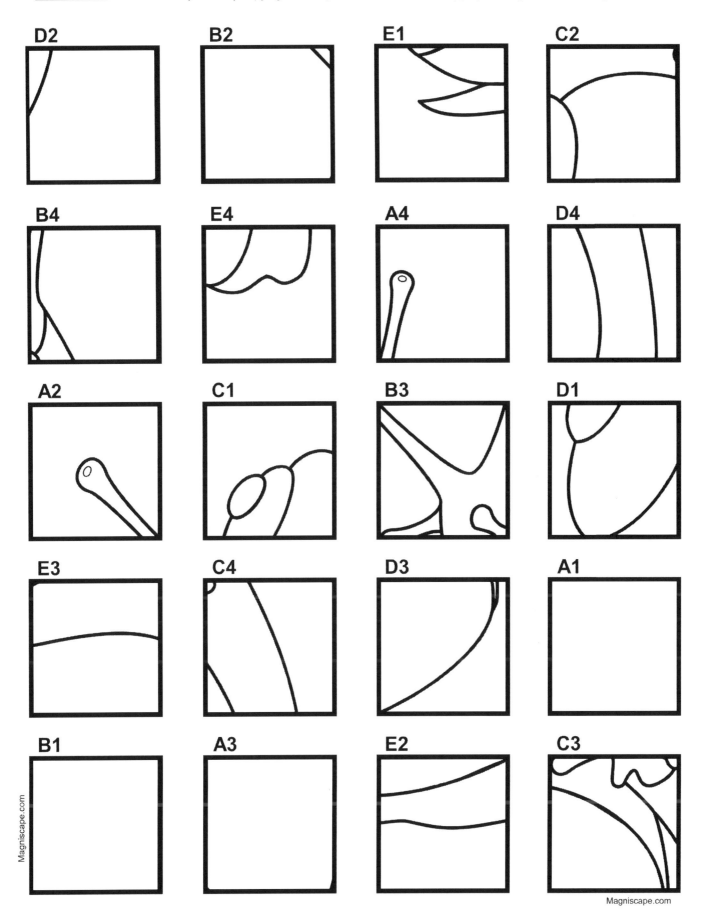

D2 B2 E1 C2

B4 E4 A4 D4

A2 C1 B3 D1

E3 C4 D3 A1

B1 A3 E2 C3

Magniscape.com

Magniscape.com

Drawing #5 - What is it?

Instructions: Recreate the picture by copying the components below into the appropriate squares on blank grid sheet #5.

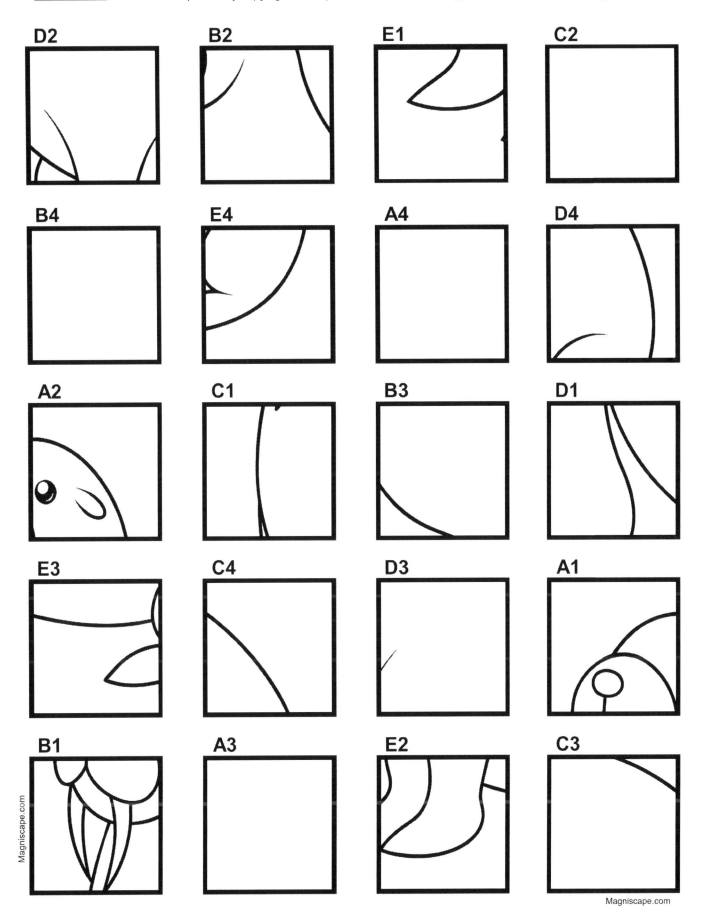

Drawing #6 - **What is it?**

<u>**Instructions:**</u> Recreate the picture by copying the components below into the appropriate squares on blank grid sheet #6.

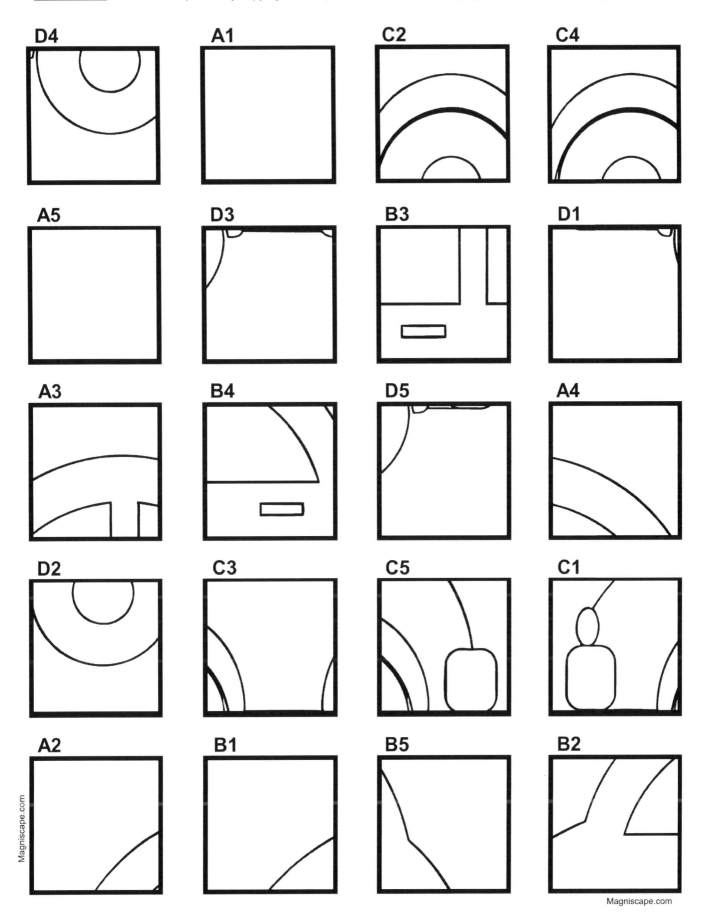

Drawing #7 - What is it?

Instructions: Recreate the picture by copying the components below into the appropriate squares on blank grid sheet #6.

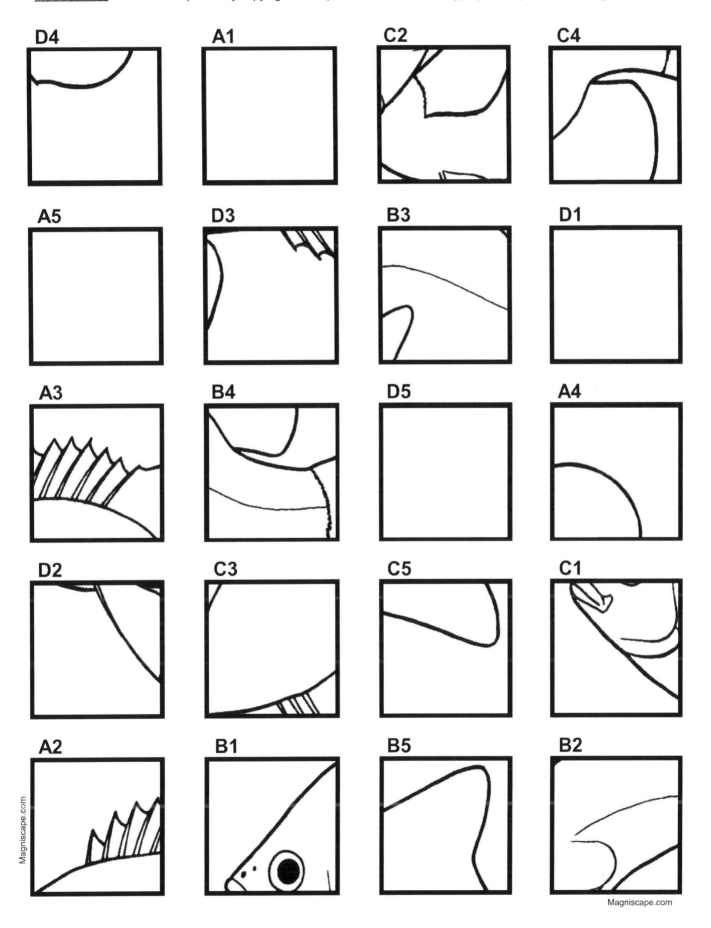

Drawing #8 - What is it?

Instructions: Recreate the picture by copying the components below into the appropriate squares on blank grid sheet #6.

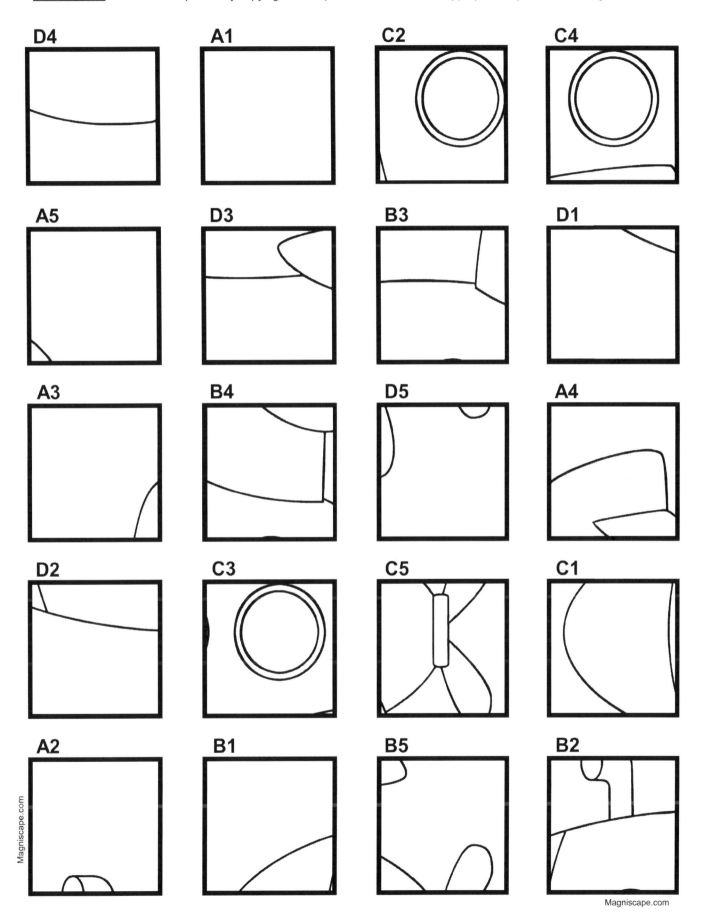

Drawing #9 - What is it?

Instructions: Recreate the picture by copying the components below into the appropriate squares on blank grid sheet #6.

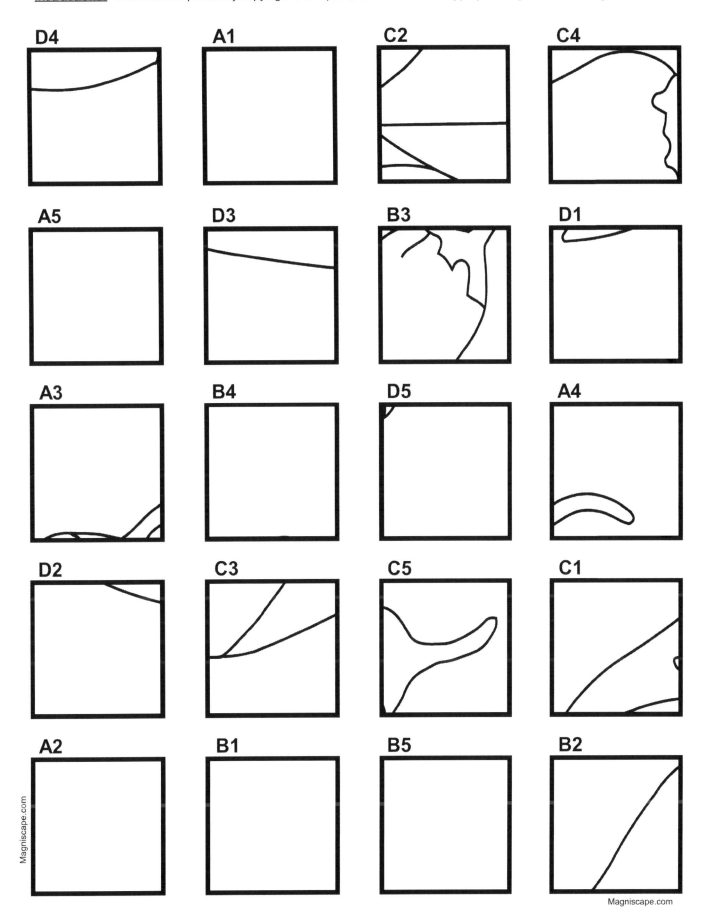

Drawing #10 - What is it?

Instructions: Recreate the picture by copying the components below into the appropriate squares on blank grid sheet #6.

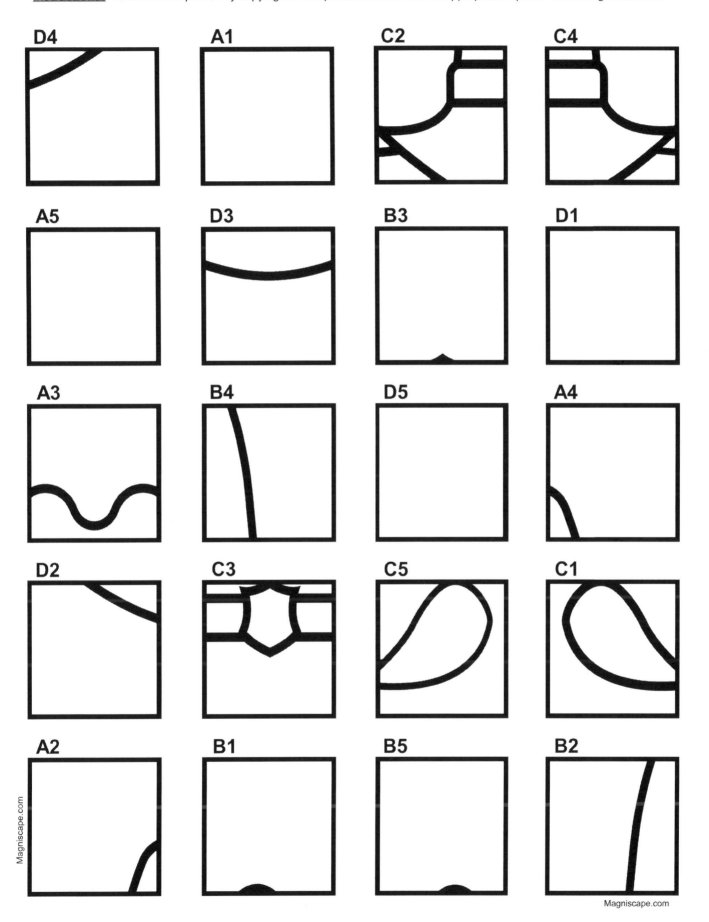

Magniscape.com

Magniscape.com

Drawing #11 - What is it?

Instructions: Recreate the picture by copying the components below into the appropriate squares on blank grid sheet #3.

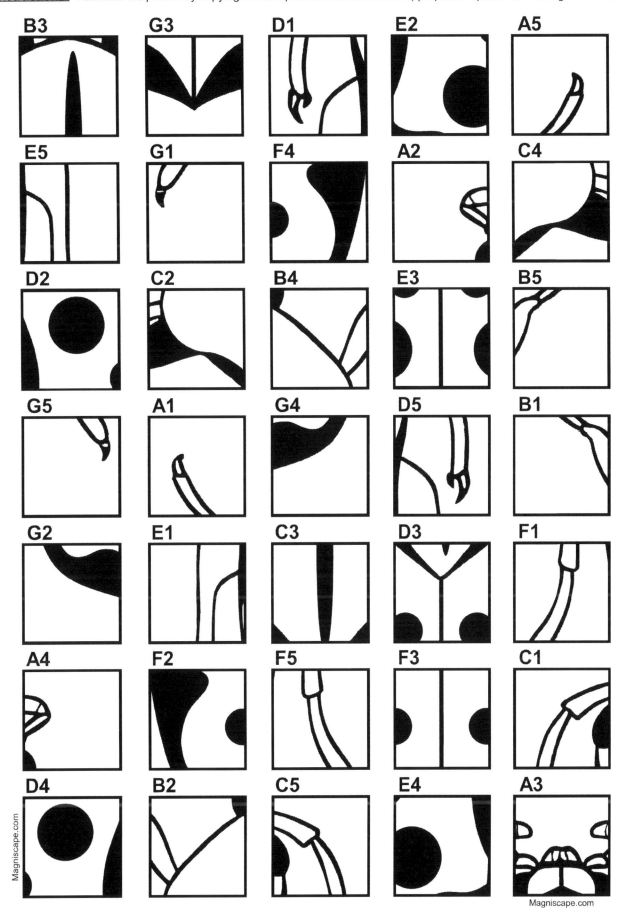

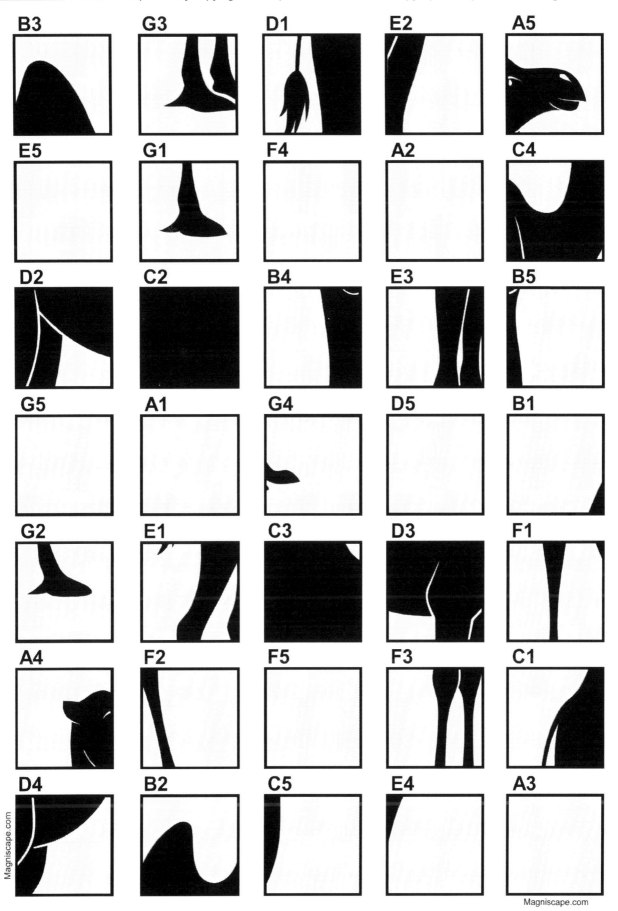

Magniscape.com

Magniscape.com

Magniscape.com

Magniscape.com

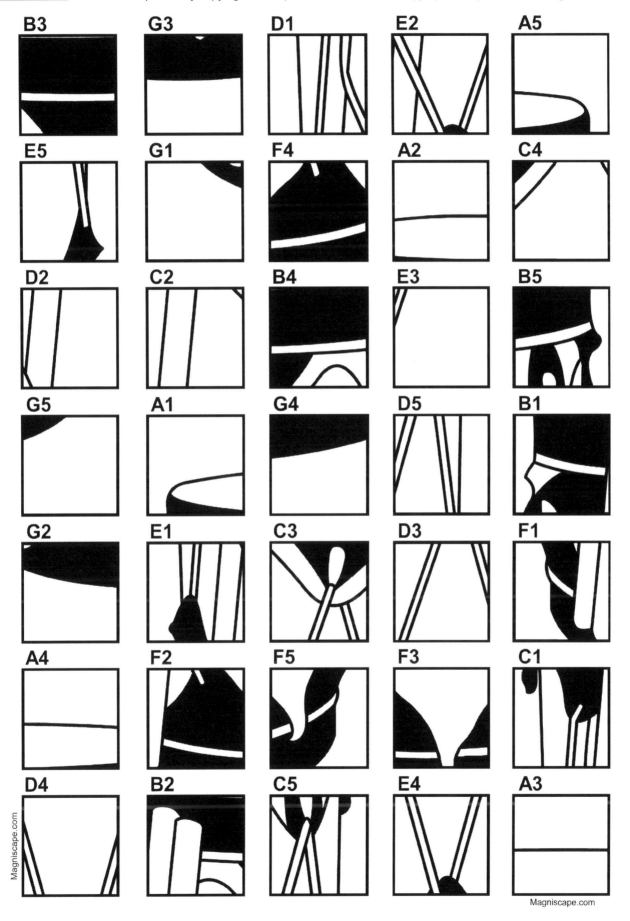

Drawing #16 - What is it?

Instructions: Recreate the picture by copying the components below into the appropriate squares on blank grid sheet #3.

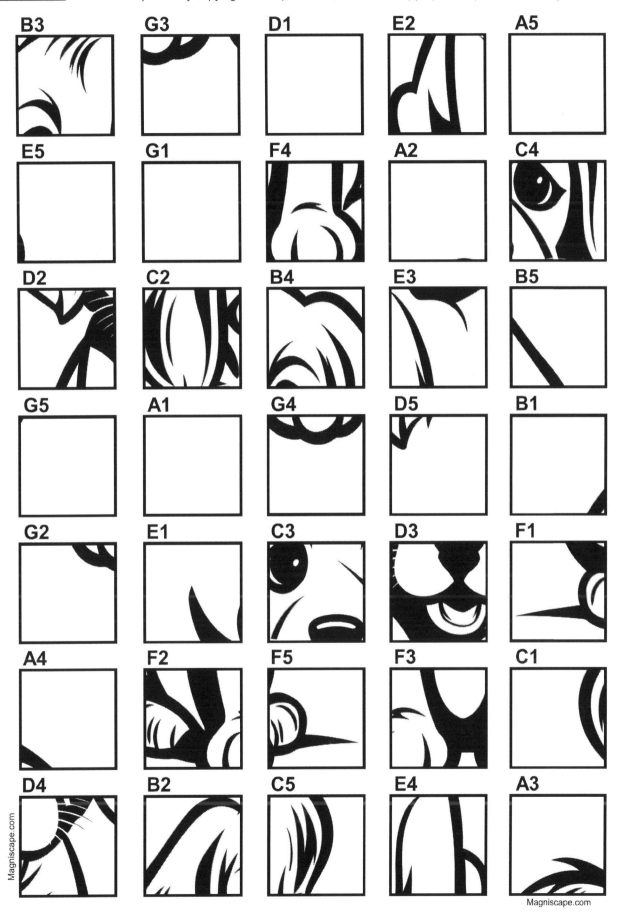

Drawing #17 - What is it?

Instructions: Recreate the picture by copying the components below into the appropriate squares on blank grid sheet #3.

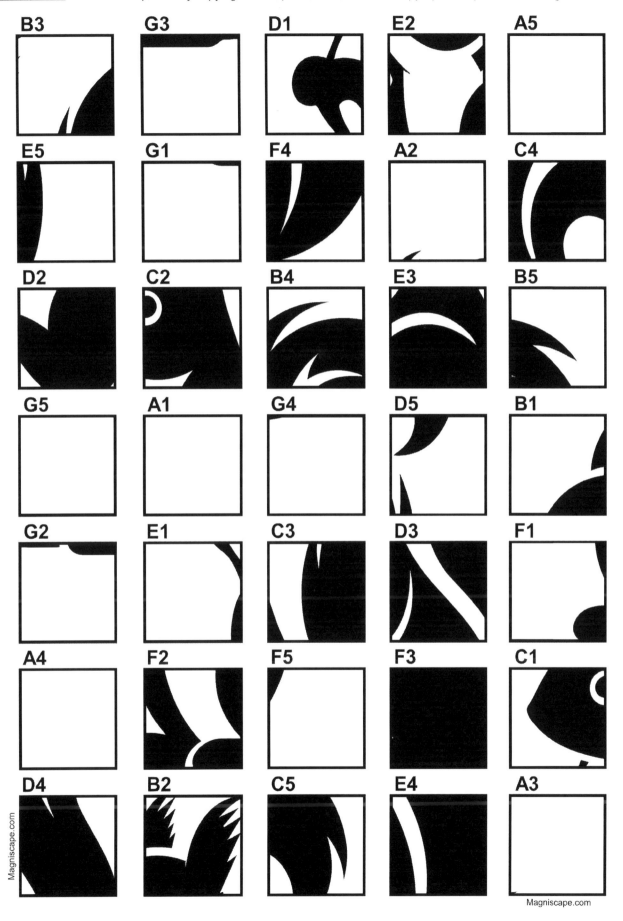

Drawing #18 - What is it?

Instructions: Recreate the picture by copying the components below into the appropriate squares on blank grid sheet #3.

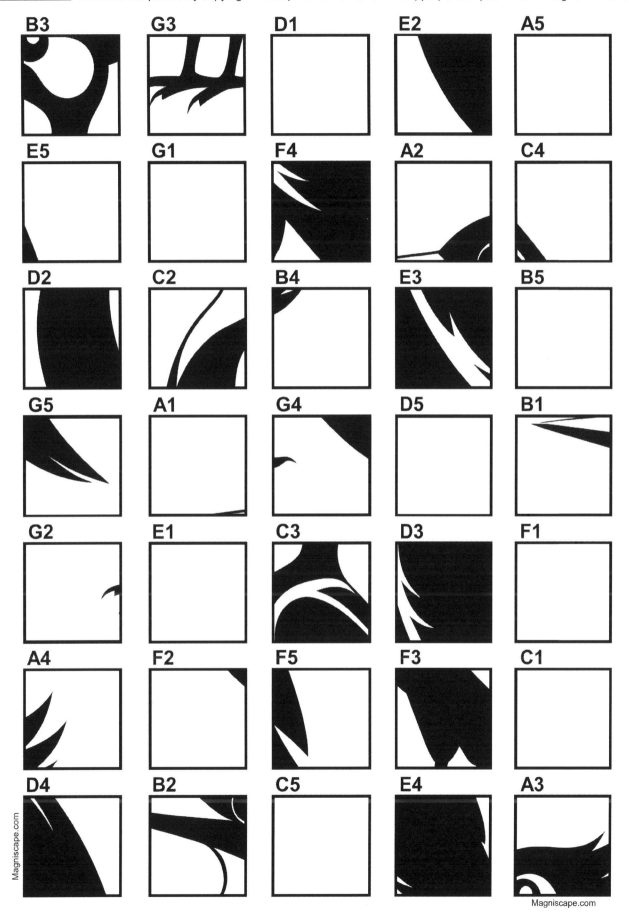

Drawing #20 - What is it?

Instructions: Recreate the picture by copying the components below into the appropriate squares on blank grid sheet #4.

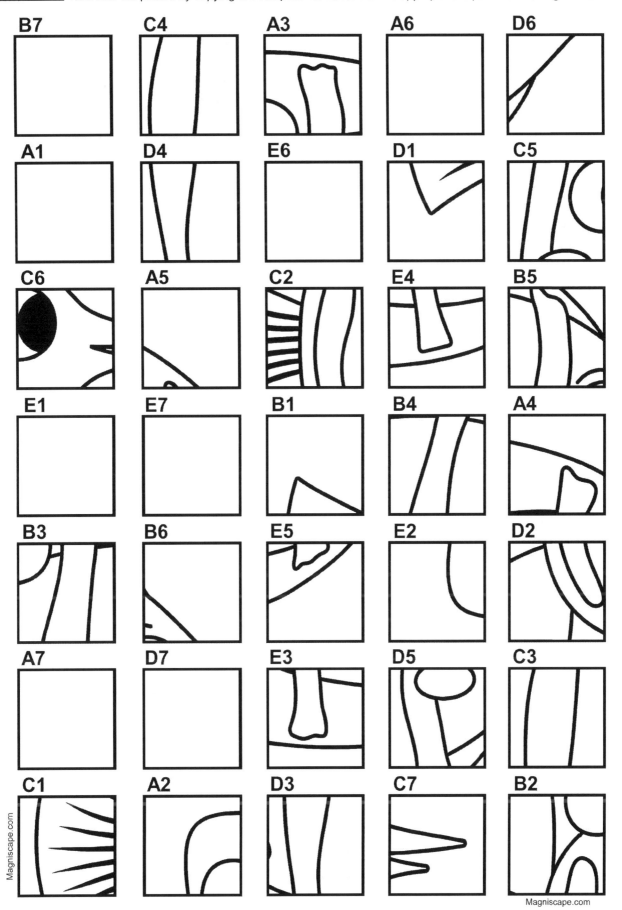

Drawing #21 - What is it?

Instructions: Recreate the picture by copying the components below into the appropriate squares on blank grid sheet #1.

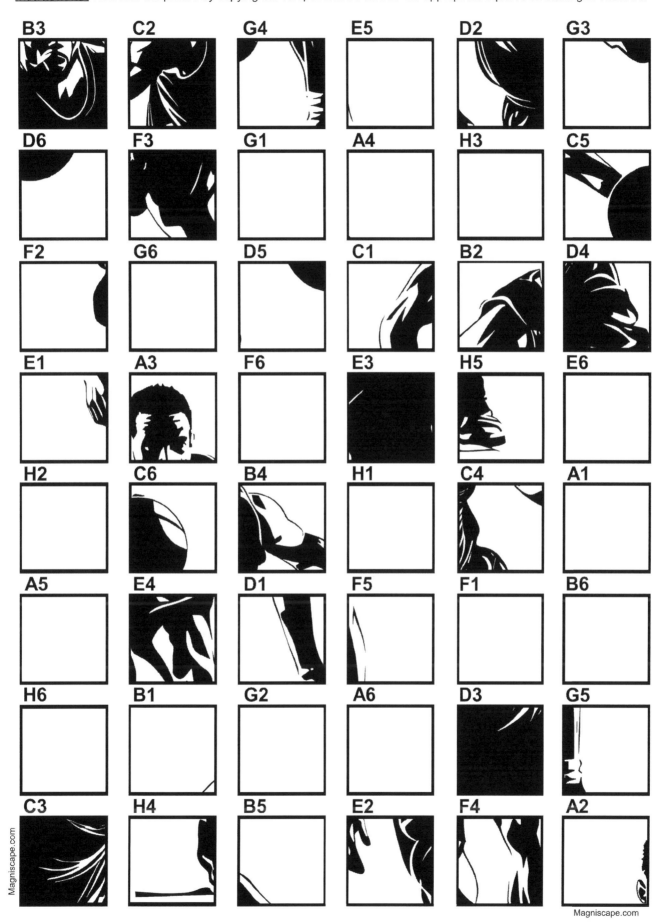

Drawing #22 - What is it?

Instructions: Recreate the picture by copying the components below into the appropriate squares on blank grid sheet #1.

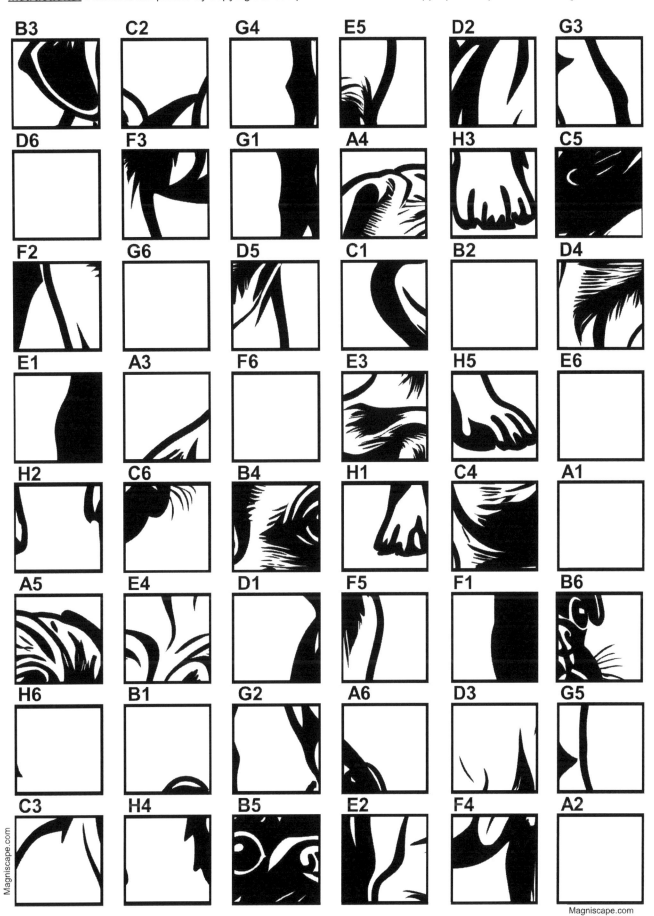

Magniscape.com

Magniscape.com

Drawing #23 - What is it?

Instructions: Recreate the picture by copying the components below into the appropriate squares on blank grid sheet #2.

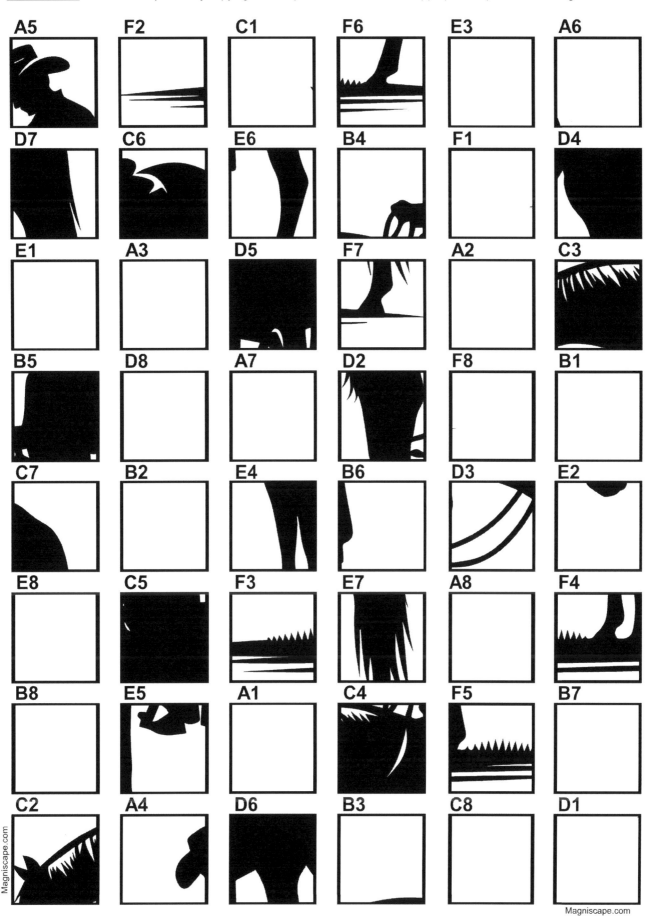

Instructions: Recreate the picture by copying the components below into the appropriate squares on blank grid sheet #2.

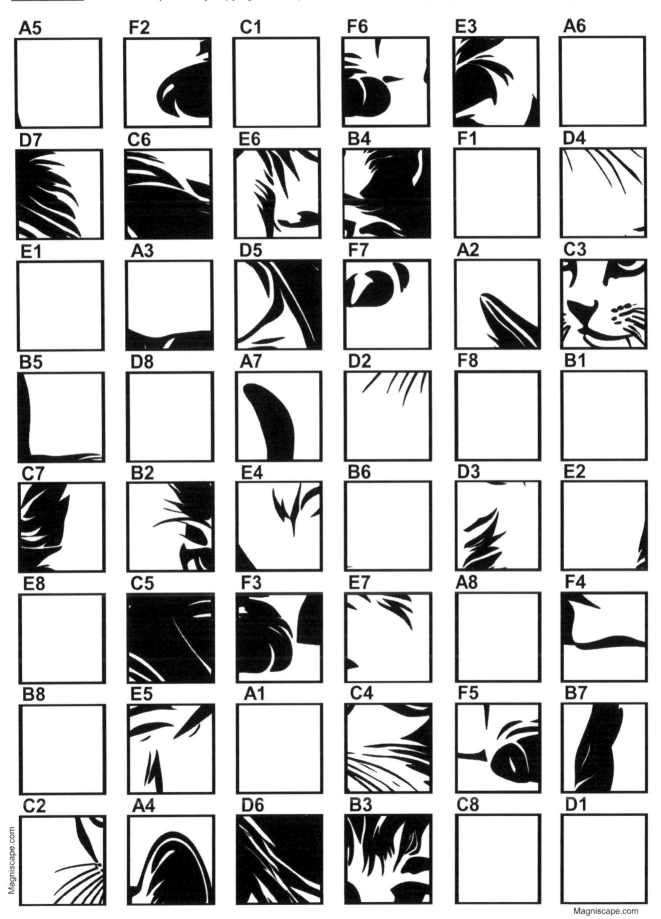

Drawing #25 - What is it?

Instructions: Recreate the picture by copying the components below into the appropriate squares on blank grid sheet #2.

Drawing #26 - What is it?

Instructions: Recreate the picture by copying the components below into the appropriate squares on blank grid sheet #1.

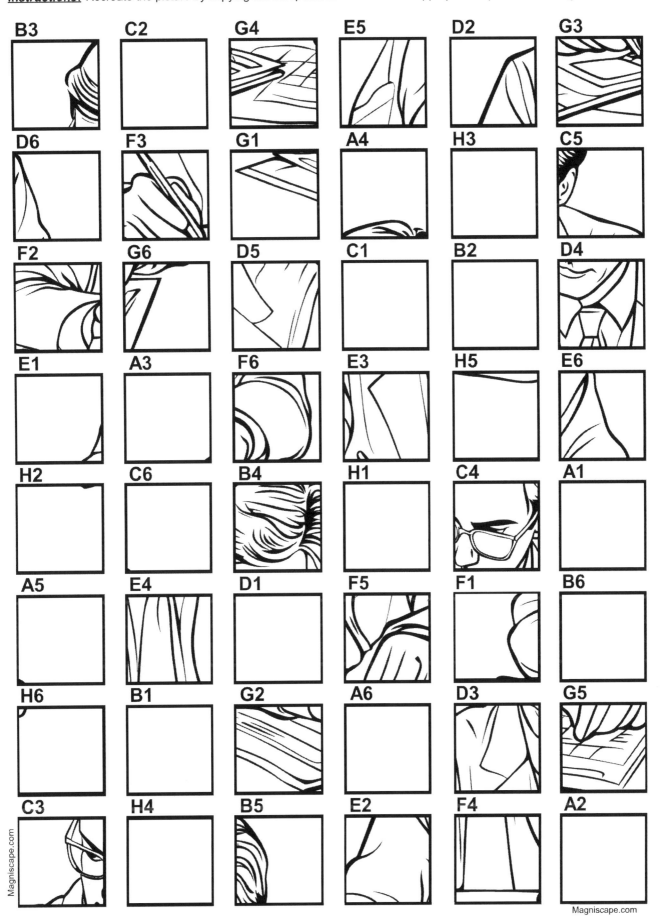

Instructions: Recreate the picture by copying the components below into the appropriate squares on blank grid sheet #2.

Drawing #28 - What is it?

Instructions: Recreate the picture by copying the components below into the appropriate squares on blank grid sheet #2.

Magniscape.com

Magniscape.com

Drawing #29 – What is it?

Instructions: Recreate the picture by copying the components below into the appropriate squares on blank grid sheet #1.

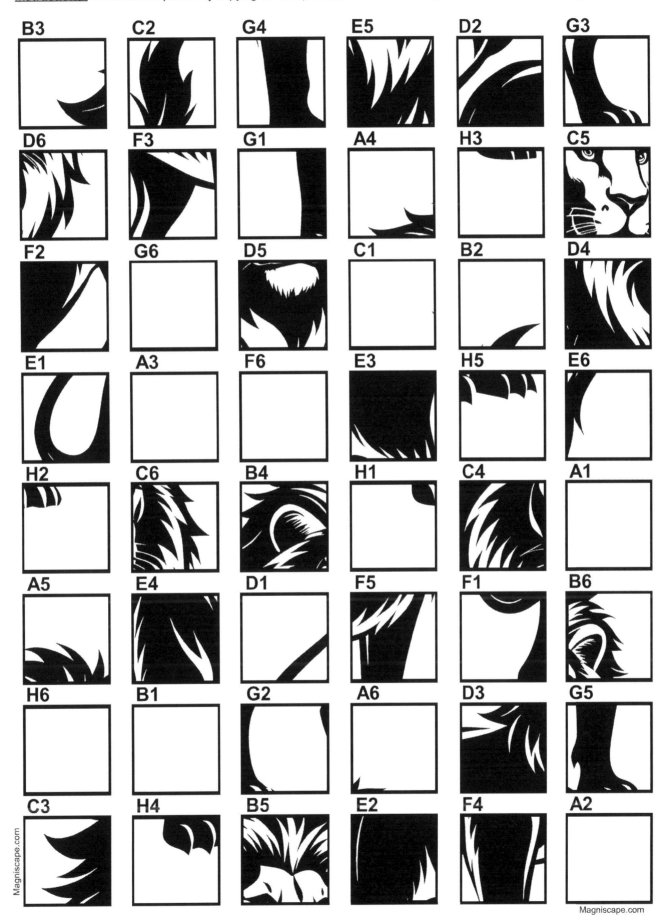

Drawing #30 - What is it?

Instructions: Recreate the picture by copying the components below into the appropriate squares on blank grid sheet #2.

Finished (Simple) Images

Drawing 1
Basketball

Drawing 2
Puppy

Drawing 3
Sailboat

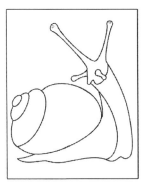

Drawing 4
Snail

Drawing 5
Walrus

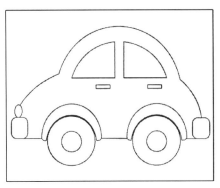

Drawing 6
Car

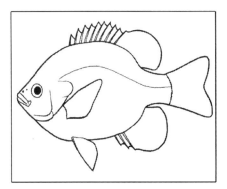

Drawing 7
Fish

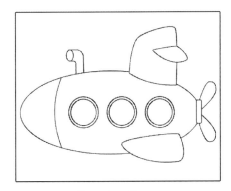

Drawing 8
Submarine

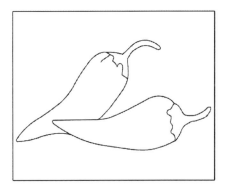

Drawing 9
Chile

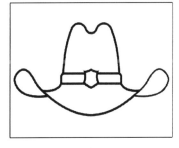

Drawing 10
Hat

Magniscape.com

Finished (Intermediate) Images

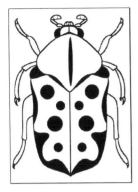

Drawing 11
Bug

Drawing 12
Camel

Drawing 13
Cat

Drawing 14
Dog

Drawing 15
Drum

Drawing 16
Puppy

Drawing 17
Squirrel

Drawing 18
Woodpecker

Drawing 19
Chicken

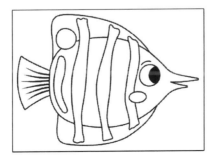

Drawing 20
Fish

Magniscape.com

Finished (Advanced) Images

Drawing 21
Basketball Player

Drawing 22
Dog

Drawing 23
Cowboy

Drawing 24
Kitten

Drawing 25
Bull

Drawing 26
Accountant

Drawing 28
Zebra

Drawing 27
Rooster

Drawing 30
Car

Drawing 29
Lion

Magniscape.com

	1	2	3	4	5	6
A						
B						
C						
D						
E						
F						
G						
H						

Grid Sheet #1

	1	2	3	4	5	6
A						
B						
C						
D						
E						
F						
G						
H						

Grid Sheet #1

	1	2	3	4	5	6
A						
B						
C						
D						
E						
F						
G						
H						

Grid Sheet #1

	1	2	3	4	5	6
A						
B						
C						
D						
E						
F						
G						
H						

Grid Sheet #1

	1	2	3	4	5	6	7	8
A								
B								
C								
D								
E								
F								

Grid Sheet #2

	A	B	C	D	E	F
1						
2						
3						
4						
5						
6						
7						
8						

Grid Sheet #2

	A	B	C	D	E	F
1						
2						
3						
4						
5						
6						
7						
8						

Grid Sheet #2

	A	B	C	D	E	F
1						
2						
3						
4						
5						
6						
7						
8						

Grid Sheet #2

	A	B	C	D	E	F
1						
2						
3						
4						
5						
6						
7						
8						

	A	B	C	D	E	F
1						
2						
3						
4						
5						
6						
7						
8						

	1	2	3	4	5
A					
B					
C					
D					
E					
F					
G					

Grid Sheet #3

Magniscape.com

	1	2	3	4	5
A					
B					
C					
D					
E					
F					
G					

Grid Sheet #3

Magniscape.com

	1	2	3	4	5
A					
B					
C					
D					
E					
F					
G					

Grid Sheet #3

	1	2	3	4	5
A					
B					
C					
D					
E					
F					
G					

Grid Sheet #3

Magniscape.com

	1	2	3	4	5
A					
B					
C					
D					
E					
F					
G					

Grid Sheet #3

Magniscape.com

	1	2	3	4	5
A					
B					
C					
D					
E					
F					
G					

Grid Sheet #3

	1	2	3	4	5
A					
B					
C					
D					
E					
F					
G					

Grid Sheet #3

	1	2	3	4	5
A					
B					
C					
D					
E					
F					
G					

Grid Sheet #3

	1	2	3	4	5
A					
B					
C					
D					
E					
F					
G					

Grid Sheet #3

	1	2	3	4	5	6	7
A							
B							
C							
D							
E							

	1	2	3	4
A				
B				
C				
D				
E				

Grid Sheet #5

Magniscape.com

	1	2	3	4
A				
B				
C				
D				
E				

Grid Sheet #5

Magniscape.com

	1	2	3	4
A				
B				
C				
D				
E				

Grid Sheet #5

	1	2	3	4
A				
B				
C				
D				
E				

Grid Sheet #5

Magniscape.com

	1	2	3	4
A				
B				
C				
D				
E				

Grid Sheet #5

Grid Sheet #6

	A	B	C	D
1				
2				
3				
4				
5				

	1	2	3	4	5
A					
B					
C					
D					

A   1

B   2

C   3

D   4

    5

	A	B	C	D
1				
2				
3				
4				
5				

	A	B	C	D
1				
2				
3				
4				
5				

Made in the USA
Las Vegas, NV
11 December 2024

13775194R00072